GO FORTH AND TELL

THE LIFE OF AUGUSTA BAKER, LIBRARIAN AND MASTER STORYTELLER

Written by BREANNA J. MCDANIEL

illustrated by APRIL HARRISON

DIAL BOOKS FOR YOUNG READERS

Augusta Braxton Baker grew up to be a master storyteller.
But before that, she was an amazing story *listener.*

Growing up in Baltimore,
it didn't matter whether she was

sitting at the
kitchen table,

walking to
the store,

GROCERY

or relaxing under a tree.

When her storytelling
grandmother started
her tales, Augusta
stopped, stuck out
her eager ears,
and listened.

Her grandmother's lilting, tilting voice shaped
incredible worlds and passed them down to Augusta.

Through that voice she traveled to where
Br'er Rabbit laughed in briar patches and
where Arthur gallivanted with Excalibur.

In these worlds, people who started out discarded and mistreated became heroes who slayed dragons or used their smarts to get themselves out of trouble!

These stories taught Augusta that where there's a will, there's a way. And she never, ever forgot that.

Augusta was enchanted by words and the way
they could change how she thought and learned.
Could she become a storyteller too? Could her stories
help other people become better listeners?

Higgledy

JUNGLE

GOLDEN

Odyssey

imagine

STORY

TELLING

Believe

Whistle

TALES

RESPECT THAT RUNNETH DEEP
A LOVE WITHOUT BOUNDARIES
A COMMON GROUND WE SHARE
WE ARE THE OTHERS KEEPER

WE ARE THE TIES THAT BIND
A HERITAGE OF KINSHIP
OF THE MOST PHENOMENAL KIND
OUR LOVE IS COMPLEX

It was time to find out.

Augusta pocketed her grandmother's stories and took her own lilting, tilting voice to a teacher's college in Albany, New York.

In school, one of her teachers taught a lesson on folk stories.

Augusta's grandmother's tales jumped joyfully to the front of her mind, and Augusta knew they were part of a bigger story—

A story of movement and courage.
The tales begged to be plucked from her memories and retold.

Augusta knew that her calling was to be in front of a crowd, raising her voice and guiding children of all ages through the wide and wonderful spaces of her stories.

That calling took her to the 135th Street Branch of the New York Public Library in Harlem, where Augusta became a children's librarian, happily sharing stories with others in her community.

Many of the children Augusta served in Harlem were African American. But there were hardly any books with Black people in them.

The ones that the library did have were
RUDE, MEAN, and JUST PLAIN WRONG.

Augusta realized there was a lot of work
to do, but where there's a will, there's a way!

Boomba

A Child's Garden of Verses

Higgledy Piggledy Room

TAG-ALONG TOOLOO

Books about Negro Life

ED

A Baker's Dozen

SONDO

THE LION OF ETHIOPIA

101

THE TALKING TREE

African Folktales

Been

YOUNG YEARS

FIN

JANIE BELLE

THE HANDSOME DONKEY

BANTU

The Long

She knew that the eager, listening ears of
young, solemn JAMES BALDWIN and poetry-loving AUDRE LORDE
deserved to hear stories where they laughed and gallivanted.

She knew they could one day tell their own stories if she only showed them how.

I often wonder what I'd do if there weren't any books in the world.
JAMES BALDWIN

James Baldwin
Go Tell It on the Mountain

UNDERSONG
AUDRE LORDE

"If I didn't define myself for myself, I would be crunched into other people's fantasies for me and eaten alive."
•••
AUDRE LORDE

She decided to use her voice—not just to share the stories she already knew, but to search out new ones, and even create some of her own.

Augusta remembered how the heroes in her grandmother's stories sometimes started out at the bottom but would rise up!

She wanted Black children to have heroes that rose up and looked, talked, and shined bright, just like them.

She created the James Weldon Johnson Memorial Collection at the 135th Street Branch to showcase honest, caring depictions of Black folks, and she shared and published her lists so countless others could learn from them. She went out of her way to support educators, librarians, and writers. And they supported her too.

Educators like CARTER G. WOODSON, the "Father of Black History" and founder of Black History Month,

and librarians like Augusta's colleague in Chicago, CHARLEMAE ROLLINS, the first Black president of the American Library Association's children's division.

Carter

Charlemae

Tom

Virginia

John

Walter

Authors and artists like JOHN STEPTOE, VIRGINIA HAMILTON, TOM FEELINGS, and WALTER DEAN MYERS, who created stories for and about Black people, sharing their lives and experiences around the globe.

Eventually, Augusta became the coordinator of children's services in ALL of the New York Public Library branches. She was the very first Black person to ever hold that position.

Known as the
Mistress of Storytelling,
Augusta traveled all over the
country, gifting people her
time and her stories.

It didn't matter where she was . . .

teaching classes at Columbia University,

hosting a radio show,

or on the set at *Sesame Street*.

As one journalist said, wherever Augusta went, she "painted worlds with her words."

Full, bright worlds for the children
who make our own world whole.

In 1980 Augusta accepted a job created just for her as the master Storyteller-in-Residence at the University of South Carolina.

To this day, the city of Columbia honors her with an annual festival called A(ugusta) Baker's Dozen.

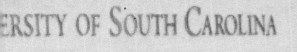

ERSITY OF SOUTH CAROLINA

There, under trees and tents with food and friends, griots and authors tell tales, shining a bright light and painting a more brilliant, bold world with their words.

Go and have a listen.

APRIL 1, 1911
Augusta Braxton is born in Baltimore, Maryland

1927
Augusta leaves home at age sixteen to start school at the University of Pittsburgh; she falls in love and marries. Her married name becomes Augusta Braxton Baker

1934
Baker becomes the first Black person to earn a degree in library sciences and information studies from SUNY Albany

1937
Baker becomes the children's librarian at the 135th Street Branch of the New York Public Library

1944
Baker curates the James Weldon Johnson Memorial collection, a group of books curated to amplify authentic representations of Black life in America

1946
Books About Negro Life for Children, a compilation of the books Baker curated in the James Weldon Johnson Memorial collection, is published

1955
Baker helps establish the children's library services for the Trinidad Public Library

1955
The Talking Tree: Fairy Tales from 15 Lands, Baker's second book, is published

1961
Baker is promoted to coordinator of children's services in all of the New York Public Library and is the first Black person to earn such a high position in the history of the NYPL

1971
Baker hosts the weekly broadcast "The World of Children's Literature" on WNYC Radio

1977
Storytelling: Art and Technique, Baker's book written with Ellin Greene on the craft of storytelling, is published

1980
Baker becomes Storyteller-in-Residence at the University of South Carolina

1987
Richland Library and the School of Information Science at the University of South Carolina inaugurate A(UGUSTA) BAKER'S DOZEN: A CELEBRATION OF STORIES, a storytelling festival for school children in Columbia, South Carolina, that continues to this day.

1998
Augusta Baker passes away and leaves a full legacy for future storytellers to follow in her light.

CITATIONS

"Augusta Baker." *Prabook.com*, https://prabook.com/web/augusta.baker/3749268.

"Augusta Braxton Baker." *Encyclopædia Britannica*, Encyclopædia Britannica, Inc., 19 Feb. 2023, https://www.britannica.com/biography/Augusta-Braxton-Baker.

"Augusta Braxton Baker—Pioneer for Black Librarianship." *GAFFNEY LEWIS LLC*, 16 Mar. 2021, https://gaffneylewis.com/augusta-braxton-baker-pioneer-for-black-librarianship/.

Baker, Augusta, and Ellin Greene. *Storytelling: Art and Technique*. R.R. Bowker, 1987.

Baker, Augusta, and Johannes Troyer. *The Talking Tree: Fairy Tales from 15 Lands*. Lippincott, 1955.

Garner, Carla. "Augusta Braxston Baker (1911–1998)." 8 Sept. 2010, https://www.blackpast.org/african-american-history/baker-augusta-braxston-1911-1998/.

Jones, Christina. "Celebrating the Legacy of Augusta Baker" *Celebrating the Legacy of Augusta Baker | Education Library*, Indiana University Bloomington, 12 Jan. 2021, https://libraries.indiana.edu/celebrating-legacy-augusta-baker.

Saxon, Wolfgang. "Augusta B. Baker, 86, Storyteller, Editor and Children's Librarian." *The New York Times*, The New York Times, 6 Mar. 1998, https://www.nytimes.com/1998/03/06/arts/augusta-b-baker-86-storyteller-editor-and-children-s-librarian.html.

Smith, Henrietta M. "An Interview with Augusta Baker." *The Horn Book*, https://www.hbook.com/story/an-interview-with-augusta-baker.

T, Rebecca. "Augusta Baker and the Art of Storytelling." *Augusta Baker and the Art of Storytelling | Richland Library*, 24 Mar. 2022, https://www.richlandlibrary.com/blog/2021-04-09/augusta-baker-and-art-storytelling.

Walker, Donna Isbell. "Augusta Baker Painted a World Using Her Words." *The Greenville News*, 1 Feb. 2015, https://www.greenvilleonline.com/story/life/2015/02/01/augusta-baker-storyteller-librarian-sesame-street/22669123/.

Williams, Robert V. "Interview with Augusta Baker." *Speaking of History: The Words of South Carolina Librarians*, http://www.libsci.sc.edu/histories/oralhistory/bakertran.htm.

AUTHOR'S NOTE

"Pardon me, Ms. Carnes? Ms. Michelle Carnes? It's me, Breanna McDaniel, from the Fairburn-Hobgood library?" My childhood librarian turned and beamed at me, laughing with the brightness that had carried me through middle school and into high school. "Oh my goodness, hello Breanna!"

In an impossible sea of people at the 2018 American Library Association's New Orleans convention, I'd managed to find Ms. Carnes and we settled into a hug that left me in tears. We embraced and exclaimed so joyfully that a stranger saw we were having "a moment" and asked if we wanted a picture.

Standing cheek-to-cheek with a woman who had known me when I was a young, passionate-about-everything girl and had, with her guidance and grace, helped me grow into the scholar and writer I am today, I fully understood why Audre Lorde adored Augusta Baker so much. Ms. Baker had taught her to read. She had saved her life, just as my own librarian had saved mine.

I've had plenty of Augusta Bakers in my life and so it was an absolute privilege to be asked to write about this incredible innovator and path maker.

Growing up, I heard "Where there's a will, there's a way" every time I tried to quit a project, activity, or conversation that seemed a little too hard. Everything about Augusta Baker's life embodies that saying for me. She graduated high school early and immediately left home for college. She believed in her dreams and refused to back down when racism and segregation tried to stop her from getting the education she wanted in New York. As a librarian, Augusta Baker refused to accept that the horrible images of Black children and Black people in the books available in her library were the only ones that existed.

Ms. Baker's will found a way to change how publishers, writers, and other librarians approached Black children's literature through her curated booklists and the stories she shared.

The people she touched at every level of her career, from Audre Lorde and James Baldwin to Ezra Jack Keats and John Steptoe, built a network of creators that paved the way for stories like mine. Her bright imagined worlds became my reality, delivered through love, care, and storytelling by folks like Ms. Carnes.

Augusta Baker always put her community first, and her stories were gifts to grateful listeners who would pocket them to share later, drawing inspiration from them forever.

Courtesy of the Photographs and Prints Division, Schomburg Center for Research in Black Culture, The New York Public Library; copyright owner unkown.

"Children of all ages want to hear stories.
Select well, prepare well and then go forth and just *tell*."

—AUGUSTA BRAXTON BAKER

For Ms. Carnes, with gratitude and care —BJM

This is dedicated to those Librarians,
like Augusta Baker, who stand in the gap
and make a positive impression on
the lives of ALL children. —AH

DIAL BOOKS FOR YOUNG READERS
An imprint of Penguin Random House LLC, New York

First published in the United States of America by Dial Books for Young Readers,
an imprint of Penguin Random House LLC, 2024

Text copyright © 2024 by Breanna J. McDaniel
Illustrations copyright © 2024 by April Harrison
Photo of Augusta Baker courtesy of the New York Public Library; copyright owner unknown.

Visit us online at PenguinRandomHouse.com.

Library of Congress Cataloging-in-Publication Data is available.

ISBN 9780593324202
10 9 8 7 6 5 4 3 2 1

Manufactured in China
TOPL

Design by Sylvia Bi
Text set in Redcurrant
Art was created using mixed media collage, acrylics and artist pens.

This is a work of nonfiction. Some names and identifying details have been changed.